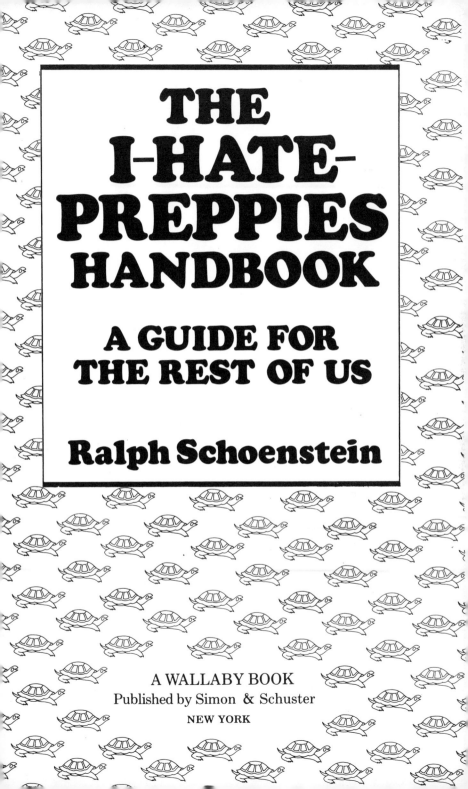

THE I-HATE-PREPPIES HANDBOOK

A GUIDE FOR THE REST OF US

Ralph Schoenstein

A WALLABY BOOK
Published by Simon & Schuster
NEW YORK

Photographs copyright © 1981 by Tom Dunham

Illustrations copyright © 1981 by Loretta Lustig

Designed by Stanley S. Drate

WALLABY and colophon are registered
trademarks of Simon & Schuster

First Wallaby Books Printing August 1981
10 9 8 7 6 5 4 3 2 1
Manufactured in the United States of America

ISBN 0-671-43796-8

For
Judy, Jill, Eve-Lynn, and Lori
The best group of all

Contents

There Are No Words

Many people helped in the making of this book, none of whom was my editor. I must, therefore, acknowledge these people for sharing not only in the production of the book but, even more important, in the blame.

For invaluable assistance with source material and spelling, I thank Phil Billington, Phil Rizzuto, Sam White, Alexander Haig, Adam Roth, Dave Howard, Fats Domino, John Dean, Jill Schoenstein, Jonas Salk, Pierre Trudeau, Laurie Boyd, Eve-Lynn Schoenstein, Kurt Waldheim, Rosemary Wren, Joe Scavone, Jeffrey Artenstein, and the estate of Fatty Arbuckle.

All of these people have graciously asked that their names not be used.

Preface

In America today, the alligator is hardly an endangered species, for he sits on millions of chests, just below the supercilious swamp of the Preppie's mind. Millions of other Americans, however, have only soy sauce on their shirts; they lack both the money and stuffiness to be Preps; and they fit into four major Anti-Prep groups, each as distinctive, demanding, and depressing as the Preps.

This book is a celebration of these people who are neither as tight-assed nor as nasal as the Preps, people joyously open at both ends. As our economy slowly sinks in the west, it seems to me that more and more students, as well as more and more backward adults, will be wanting to leave their lodges, clubs, and klans and join these groups, in which mummy means only an old Egyptian.

The American public high school is as structured as an anthill, though not as intelligent, of course; and because this school has never been a melting pot (although melting pot is the one thing students haven't yet tried doing with it), certain generalizations about Greasers, Jocks, Freaks, and Nerds will be made in this book and some of them will be offensive. At least, that is my hope, for my research has been exhaustive—I got tired ten minutes after it began—and my goal has been nothing less than the anthropological profundity of *The Coming of Age in Samoa* and *Texas Christian Tramp.*

Americans have long been yearning to know more about these four Anti-Prep groups than what appears on TV because the kids in these groups occasionally mature and become the heart of our nation, the people who end up fixing our cars and our Congressmen.

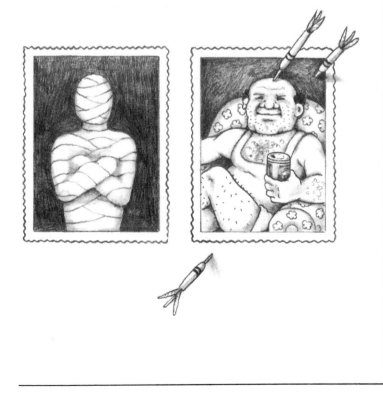

A BRIEF HISTORY OF ANTI-PREPPINESS

Preppiness, of course, was invented by General Robert E. Lee, who had a tailgate party for his staff at a wagon just before the Battle of Bull Run.

"We'll beat the North," Lee said, "because they're such a tacky crowd. Rotten clothes and wrong schools."

The first Greaser, however, was not General Grant, even though he loved to spit.

Here are brief histories of the four Anti-Prep groups, prepared with the help of the Library of Congress and the Bureau of Missing Persons.

Jock

Contrary to popular opinion, the work Jock is not derived from the term athletic supporter. *Nothing* is derived from an athletic supporter except shrunken testicles, but that is the subject of some other book. The word Jock comes from Jacques Schneiderman, a 1946 graduate of DeWitt Clinton High, who played five varsity sports with dynamic ineptitude, but who always smelled of after-shave and who always carried a small canvas bag, which contained bagels and medical photographs of young girls.

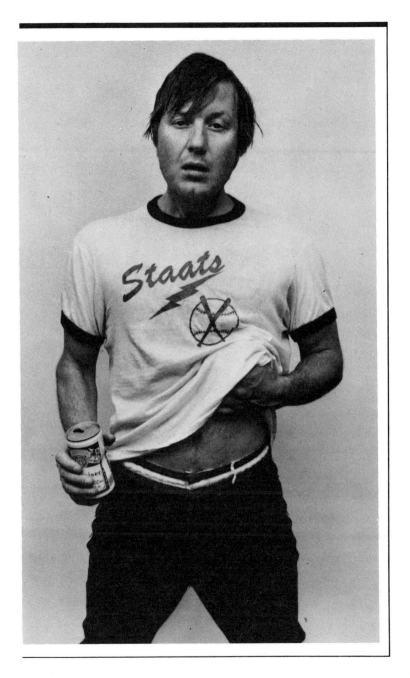

Greaser

Once again contrary to popular opinion, the word Greaser is not derived from grease, which Greasers stopped using in the spring of '63. Greaser instead goes way back, like a Greaser's hair. The word comes all the way from ancient Athens, where one of Socrates' students, Nick, dropped out of school to open a chariot repair shop.

"Nick has brought shame to Athens," said another student to Socrates.

"Yes," Socrates replied. "I wish he weren't a Greecer."

Freak

Freak does not mean a woman who can use her navel to launch sesame seeds. The word is a shortening of Drug Freak; but it also includes miscellaneous weirdos, like lovers of wheat germ and Japanese whales. The first American Freak was a member of the Continental Congress named Eugene Brissie, who found a way to mainline snuff and as late as 1802 was asking how the war had come out.

Nerd

This is the only group that goes back to Biblical days, when making flour was a compulsory course. There were always a few students who made more flour than necessary and they became known as Grinders—shortened in the 14th century to Grinds and in the 17th to Nerds by someone who couldn't shorten too well. Two distinct kinds of Nerds are indigenous to America today: the asshole with a high IQ and the asshole with a low one. The difference cannot be detected merely by watching the ways that they fall down.

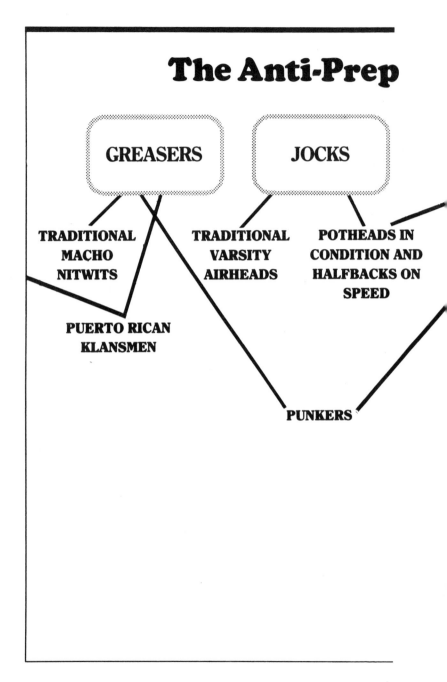

The Anti-Prep

GREASERS

JOCKS

TRADITIONAL
MACHO
NITWITS

TRADITIONAL
VARSITY
AIRHEADS

POTHEADS IN
CONDITION AND
HALFBACKS ON
SPEED

PUERTO RICAN
KLANSMEN

PUNKERS

22

Establishment

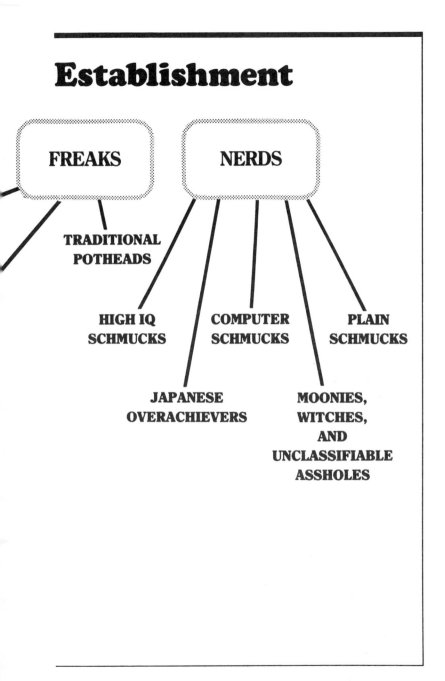

FREAKS

NERDS

TRADITIONAL
POTHEADS

HIGH IQ
SCHMUCKS

COMPUTER
SCHMUCKS

PLAIN
SCHMUCKS

JAPANESE
OVERACHIEVERS

MOONIES,
WITCHES,
AND
UNCLASSIFIABLE
ASSHOLES

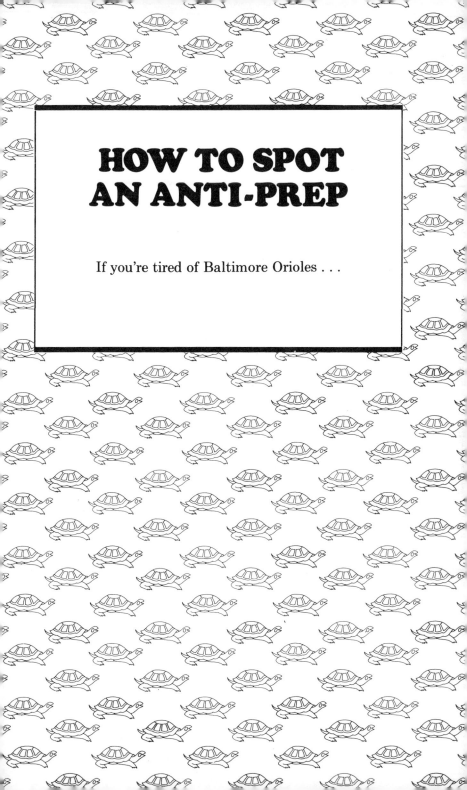

HOW TO SPOT
AN ANTI-PREP

If you're tired of Baltimore Orioles . . .

Anti-Prep Chic

Is Anti-Prep fashion the same kind of contradiction in terms as honest landlord or impoverished orthodontist? No, Anti-Prep fashion does exist and it is as widespread as athlete's foot.

To be fashionably Anti-Prep, you will need a certain basic wardrobe and accessories, depending on which of the four groups you are in—or trying to enter.

Most of the following elegant items can be purchased in the designer original section of your Army & Navy Store.

Jock

A small canvas bag, which is to be carried constantly, even to prayer, sex, and other pregame rituals.

A hip flask full of water for keeping the hair stylishly wet.

A windbreaker with a varsity letter, the name of the school, and a picture of its animal mascot—e.g., the Tigers, the Bears, the Newts.

A pair of tight, straight-legged Levis and a pair of white Pumas for strutting along.

Some pancake makeup for enriching a tan (optional for blacks).

Greaser

An Army fatigue jacket decorated with clusters of pizza stains.

A dime for calling a lawyer.

A pair of Pro-Keds or black leather shoes for shuffling along.

Shiny black leather pants and pink sweaters, mostly for girls.

Openers for bottles, cans, and cars.

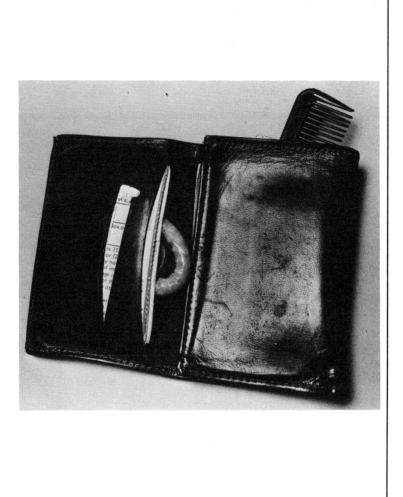

Freak

No bra—either for girls or boys—and long peasant skirts (sometimes made by Indians) that are washed once a year.

An army fatigue jacket, possibly Turkish, and always a good fit for someone else.

A blue work shirt over a Grateful Dead T-shirt over clammy skin.

A pair of sunglasses for protecting any parts of the eyes still open.

A suede belt purse for carrying joints, a guide to Colombia, and a SAVE THE SQUID button.

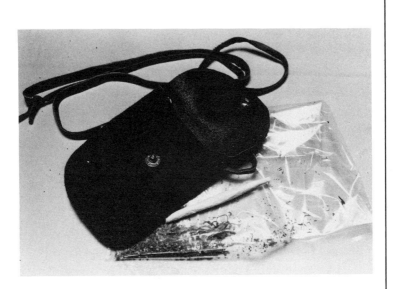

Nerd

A pair of black corrective shoes worn with sagging white socks.

A black vinyl attaché case containing three weeks of homework done in advance and an extra credit paper on how to raise diphtheria at home.

A roll of black electrician's tape for mending a crack in the frame of the glasses that will be made by walking into a wall.

Polyester pants bunched at the belt.

Six Bic pens in a plastic shirt pocket holder saying ALOHA, ASBURY PARK.

Dressing Badly to A Different Drummer

Ever since the moment of my birth, when I heard the nurse say, "Mummy, it's a boy, I think," I knew that if I was ever able to find an identity, it would have to be as an Anti-Prep.

There was, I admit, a certain amount of Preppiness in my family. My sister had legs like field hockey sticks and my father liked to go to Bermuda and drink gin. Of course, he also liked to stay in the Bronx and drink gin because he was devoted to my mother and didn't want her drinking alone.

"Father," I said to him one day, "I don't want to become a Prep. What else is there?"

"Human being," he replied, and I was launched.

In kindergarten, I became a Greaser by burping a lot, playing only with trucks, and jumping on little girls. I was happy in this group and I might have remained a Greaser had I not learned how to read and write.

It was in high school, however, that I knew I would always have to be an independent Anti-Prep. The Freaks were not yet born; the Jocks were simply Greasers who went out for teams; and the Nerds were just beyond my reach. I tried to be a Nerd by going out for the school chess team. And I might have made it had I just been able to remember how the pawn moved.

Greasers have to study too.

The Best Stores

Almost any store that deals in Formosan imports with no questions asked is fit to dress an Anti-Prep. A select few stores, however, have even lower standards than the rest and are therefore noted by us here:

Anthony's Army & Navy
Akron, Ohio

Ernie's Thrift Shop
Taos, New Mexico

Sam's Slightly Used
Utica, New York

The Rescue Mission
Trenton, New Jersey

A Mother's Guide

How can a mother tell if her baby is a blooming Greaser, Jock, Nerd, or Freak? The Anti-Prep Studies Division of Southwest Texas State Teachers College has devised the following tests:

If the child spends most of his time smiling for no apparent reason, he will probably become a Freak, especially if he also falls asleep while talking.

If he wants to be nursed at the age of twelve, a little Greaser is at hand, so to speak.

If he is competitive enough to want to be the first child on the block to be toilet trained, he is certainly a budding Jock.

And if it looks as though he will never be toilet trained, say hello to a Nerd.

An Anti-Prep by Any Other Name

Muffie is *always* the name of a Prep (or a basset hound), but sometimes we cannot determine an Anti-Prep's group just by his name and we have to use some other guide, like his breath.

For example, Al is usually a Greaser's name. But what about Al Einstein, the most distinguished twentieth century Nerd?

You see my point, even if I can't: the least scientific thing in this book is the identification of a type by his name. Keeping in mind, therefore, that the following list is almost totally worthless, here are some Anti-Prep names taken at random from the men's room in Pennsylvania Station.

Male Greasers
Tony, Joey, and Mike

Female Greasers
Toni, Joey, and Mike

Male Nerds
Newton, Seymour, and Maurice

Female Nerds
Rhoda, Ronda, Rona, and Kimiko

Male Jocks
Jack, Greg, Tug, Pug, and Fug

Female Jocks
Sue, Ellen, and Sue-Ellen

Male Freaks
Claude, Dennis, and Speed

Female Freaks
Faith, Hope, Charity, and Velocity

An American child at the crossroads. Is she becoming a Greaser, a Jock, or a Freak?

In the words of Wordsworth, "The child is the father to the man. And what a mother that man can be."

PHOTO QUIZ #1

This book will contain some tests—besides, of course, the constant one of how to understand it.

Here is Photo Quiz #1. In two days or less, find the Anti-Prep home. Do not hesitate to guess because this question will be marked on a curve.

ZOOLOGY

Where do Anti-Preps fit on the great scale of life?
Would James Herriot make a house call to one?

Heritage

We know that Preps are bred by other Preps, but who gives birth to Anti-Preps? People with something to answer for, that's who. People like these:

Nerd breeding
Nerds always come from other Nerds, although occasional ones are produced by the Yale Club and the PLO.

Jock breeding
Jocks also come from Jocks—and often prematurely because their mothers jump up and down on the sidelines so much.

Greaser breeding
Like Nerds and Jocks, Greasers almost always come from other Greasers and are born loving the right to life.

Freak breeding
A Freak, on the other hand, isn't born, he is made; so a Freak can come from any type of parent except one who knows how to bring up a child.

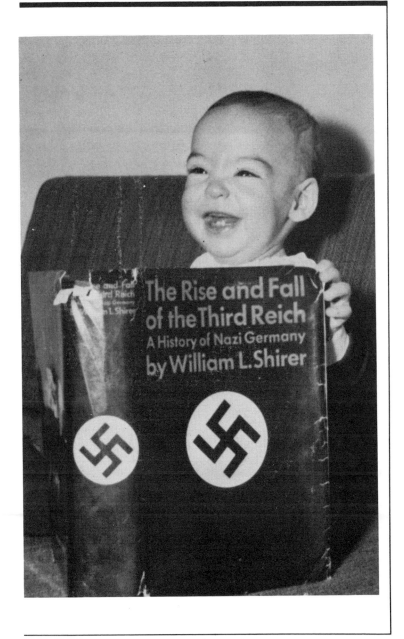

The Anti-Prep is born with good taste.

Finding Your Identity

If, at this point in the book, you still don't know in which of the Anti-Prep groups you belong, then perhaps the following in-depth test can help you place yourself.

Answer each question in fifteen minutes or less, using a number two pencil or a Snoopy crayon, and then send your answers to:

Anti-Prep Placement Service
The Menninger Clinic
Topeka, Kansas

1. If your mother were convalescing from open heart surgery, would you:
   a) Make sure she has plenty of beer
   b) Sterilize her coke spoon
   c) Challenge her to a game of racketball

2. The words Dairy Queen mean:
   a) The finest cow in the barn
   b) A gay cheese maker
   c) A nursing monarch

3. An airhead is:
   a) A jet pilot
   b) A lover of laughing gas
   c) Someone taking this test

4. Gatorade is:
   a) A drink for washing down speed
   b) Something to help a crocodile hear
   c) A network of Preps

5. Holding your middle finger in the air means:
   a) You're almost number one
   b) You're offering a resting place to a pigeon
   c) You're studying to be a weatherman

6. To "hit the books" means:
   a) To discover what the course is about
   b) To place bets with different people
   c) To fall asleep on the encyclopedia

7. Biff boff means:
   a) To have sex with Biff
   b) To have a laugh with Biff
   c) To laugh while screwing Biff

8. A "gut course" is:
   a) A course in how to string tennis rackets
   b) A course that explains the small intestine
   c) A course that requires courage to take

As American As a Kidney Punch

Of all the Anti-Prep groups, the Jock is the most purely American. Greasers are found from Naples to Nome, Freaks are adrift around the world, and three-quarters of the delegates to the United Nations are Nerds; but Jocks are always American because only America puts such stress on winning.

As Vince Lombardi so stirringly said, "Take this green one and you'll never feel it."

EDITOR'S NOTE: The author, as usual, does not know what the hell he is talking about. East Germany is even more American than America in the stress it places on winning. In fact, every *other* country is crazy about winning, too. Only Hungary seems to like coming in second.

Coffee break for a Freak.

Onward and Downward With Anti-Prep

A hybrid of the Greaser and the Freak is the Punker, the newest Anti-Prep to crawl into the sun. Punkers have no standards, so they are sometimes confused with General Motors executives. The females wear black leather jackets with silver studs, enormous earrings, and spiked heels; and the males wear black leather jackets with silver studs, enormous earrings, and spiked heels. The females, however, also like to wear black tape on their nipples, which should be removed during nursing.

Return of the Preface

Several people who learned that I was writing this book tried to stop me, not merely because they had taste but because they feared that I might be giving even more misinformation than *Time*.

"Your definitions can't be precise," one sociologist said to me. "For example, is there a difference between a Freak who experiments with studying and a Nerd who experiments with grass?"

"Of course there is," I replied. "The Nerd will put the grass on cream cheese."

Nevertheless, the sociologist did have a point; and so I suggest that you do not look to this book for all the answers, especially the capital of Vermont.

Whose Holy Land?

The geographic center of Preppiness in the United States should lie halfway between Princeton University and the Lawrenceville School. At that spot, however, is the headquarters of Squibb, sacred to the Freaks.

The claims to this holy ground by two rival sects is analogous to both Jews and Christians claiming Jerusalem or Palm Beach.

The holy city of the Nerds, of course, is Elmira, New York.

Pets

The Anti-Prep pet is less likely to be found at the Westminster Kennel Club than in a death row cell at the pound. The current favorite pets of the four groups are:

Greasers
Clydesdales

Jocks
Themselves

Freaks
Anything endangered

Nerds
Tarantulas

PHOTO QUIZ #2

Here is Photo Quiz #2. All of the following are animals, but only one is an Anti-Prep pet. Which of these would relieve himself on Muffie?

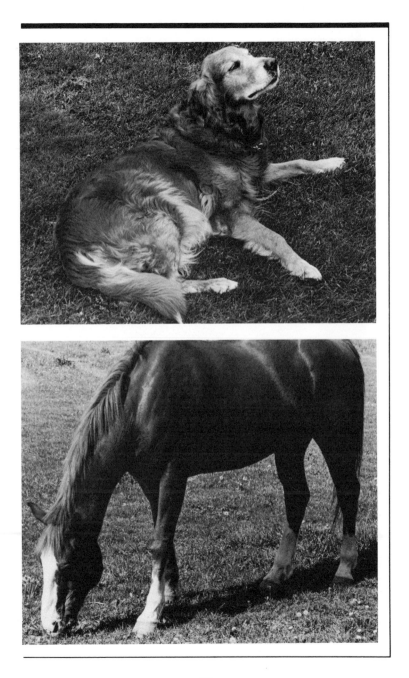

MANNERS

Should an Anti-Prep give a woman his seat on a bus? Even if he's the driver?

The Social Season

Just as a Prep feels it important to attend cotillions, reunions, and garage sales, the Anti-Prep finds certain social events obligatory too. With the gracious assistance of the style section of *The Farmers Almanac,* I have prepared a list of the top ones.

New Year's Eve

The night that Greasers like to get in their cars and pretend to drive. Not all Greasers, of course, spend New Year's Eve inside their cars. Others like to lounge in the streets, quietly drinking beer and turning in false alarms.

Ground Hog Day

The day when the Nerd comes out of the library and tries to see his shadow. If he sees it, then tradition says that he will have six more weeks of cream cheese and olive sandwiches.

Halloween

The day when a Freak has a chance to give some of the local kids flying lessons by putting hash brownies in their trick-or-treat bags. It is, of course, hard for the Freak to tell Halloween from all the other days, and so he sometimes celebrates it on September 23rd.

Easter Sunday

The day when a Jock eats turkey and gives thanks for all his blessings.

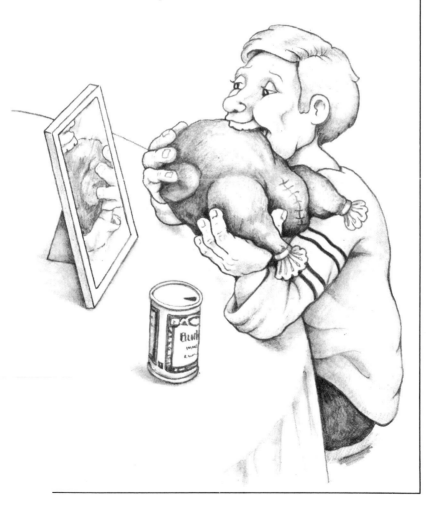

Etiquette

Are manners as important to Anti-Preps as they are to the madras and martini set? Absolutely. An Anti-Prep is deeply interested in knowing the correct fork to use for cutting his meat and the correct hand to use for scratching his ass.

Here are some pressing questions about etiquette that Ann Landers refuses to answer.

Q: If you have a Freak as a house guest and he starts sniffing the Vanish, should you politely ask him to stop?

Mona White,
Franconia Notch, New Hampshire

A: Only if he is not leaving you enough to clean the bowls.

Q: I am about to marry a Greaser who wants to honeymoon on an oil rig in the Gulf of Mexico. Is this a fashionable place to go?

Shulamit Kravitz,
Fort Sill, Oklahoma

A: Only in season.

Q: My son, a lovely Nerd, wants to open an account at a sperm bank. Is this now a sound thing to do?

Dennis Marks,
Admiral Farragut Academy

A: Yes, if he gets a toaster too.

Q: If I have Yasir Arafat to a luncheon at my club, should I seat him with the Greasers?

Lori Ravachevsky,
Reno, Nevada

A: Yes, Arafat is a Greaser, even though he prefers camels to cars.

Q: My neighbor told me that her little boy is such a great Jock that he even did some hurdling in the womb. How can I respond to this boast without calling her a liar?

Sam DuBoff,
The South Bronx

A: Better call her a liar. The only field event in the womb is a somersault.

Q: Do you have any suggestion for something to give two Greasers for a wedding present?

Peter Levin,
Santa Rosa, California

A: Find out where their muffler pattern is registered.

Decor

You can identify an Anti-Prep not only by his looks but also by his environment. Each of the four groups leans toward its own special decor—and sometimes falls over, especially after the Jock has spent an evening with Schlitz or the Freak with Boone's Farm Apple Wine or the Nerd with Manischewitz Concord Grape.

Greaser Decor

A ten-foot picture of James Dean

A collection of antique stolen hubcaps

A sign saying GUNS DON'T KILL PEOPLE, BULLETS KILL PEOPLE

Jock Decor

Sixteen *Sports Illustrated* pictures of athletes promoting victory

A picture of the Dallas Cowboys cheerleaders promoting puberty

A sign saying IF YOU CAN'T STAND THE HEAT, GET OUT OF THE SAUNA

Freak Decor

A pencil holder made from a hookah

A hookah made from a pencil holder

A sign saying DID YOU LOVE A BABY SEAL TODAY?

Nerd Decor

A centerfold from *National Geographic*

A medal for spelling from the third grade

A bronzed pair of corrective shoes

A nicely landscaped Greaser home.

Monograms

Monograms are just as important to Anti-Preps as they are to Preps, though the Anti-Prep display is subtler.

Greasers, for example, feel that it's gauche to monogram their clothing, so they monogram their skin. Not all Greasers get such monograms, of course, because some don't know their initials.

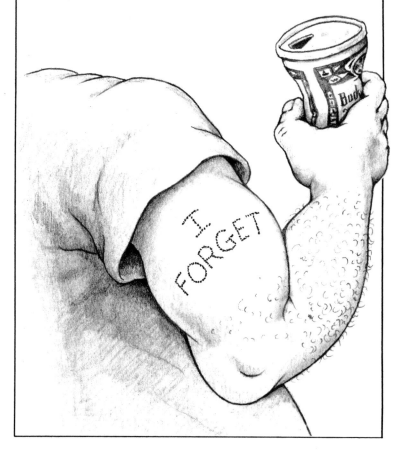

PHOTO QUIZ #3

Here is Photo Quiz #3. In the space below each meal, give the name of the Anti-Prep group that—you'll pardon the expression—eats it.

HIGHER EDUCATION

If you put a hundred Anti-Preps at typewriters,
would they eventually write *Hamlet*?
Or LIFE SUCKS?

College Life

Anti-Preps go to college. Their old school ties may be fit for Baggies, but they do go—even the Greasers, to whom attending classes has been uncool. A Greaser usually audits high school, but higher education can catch his interest because it is nice to be able to hang a diploma in the car wash.

Here, as of late yesterday morning, are the very smartest Anti-Prep schools. An SAT score in positive numbers is required for each.

For Jocks
The University of Michigan
Michigan State University
The University of California at Marina del Rey

For Greasers
Mercer County Community College
Syracuse University at Utica
The Kelman School of Refrigeration

For Nerds
The Massachusetts Institute of Technology
(sometimes known as Cal Tech)
The University of Chicago
Oral Roberts University

For Freaks
Antioch College
The New School for Social Research
The University of Beirut

The Anti-Prep Alma Mater

Oh, I wish I was in the land of cotton;
Polyester blends are rotten
And I don't
Want my Dad
In a watch
Band that's plaid.
I wish I was in Woolworth's.
Hooray!
Hooray!
In there or Grant's
My underpants
All come three for five-fifty.
And then
I'll take
Them off
When I see Dixie.

Favorite Anti-Prep Reading

Greasers
Popular Mechanics
The Cat in the Hat

Jocks
The Vince Lombardi Story
A Boy's Life of Ronald Reagan

Nerds
Fear and Trembling/The Sickness Unto Death
Radio Shack News

Freaks
High Times
Selected walls

The public library for an Anti-Prep.

The Krebs College of Cosmetology, where acne is an elective.

The Greatest Anti-Prep Heroes

The greatest Prep heroes, of course, are William F. Buckley and Emily Post. Anti-Preps, however, have their heroes too, and here is a list, prepared with the help of the research department of *The National Enquirer.*

For the Greasers
Genghis Khan

For the Nerds
Herman Kahn

For the Jocks
Clark Kent

For the Freaks
Clark Kent

RECREATION

Those moments when the Anti-Prep changes gear
from neutral to overdrive—or perhaps reverse.

Parties

Anti-Preps don't have tailgate parties, of course, because it's hard to have a tailgate party on a U-Haul. Anti-Preps, however, are starting to emulate Preps by having parties with distinctive themes. During the last social season, four themes were particularly popular:

Margaret Sanger's Birthday
Free Rudolf Hess
National Drag Queen Week
Welcome Gypsy Moths

The Anti-Prep is a man on the move.

The Anti-Prep Style of Sex

All four Anti-Prep groups recognize sex and
sometimes even reproduce, in spite of suggestions
that they don't. Their mating rituals, however, are
as different as acne and hives.

Sex for a Greaser is generally on the level of a
chimpanzee in heat, though not always that
romantic. To the Greaser, machismo is everything.
He can't spell it—in fact, he thinks that it's a new
Italian car—but he knows that there are several
people around who aren't men. The Women's
Movement has had no effect on the Greaser: to raise
a consciousness, you must be conscious to begin
with. The Greaser is an equal opportunity animal.
He would like to nail both Gloria Steinem and
Phyllis Schlafly, perhaps at the same time, in the
back of a Texaco station.

The Freak is as sexually active as the Greaser—
with one big difference. The Freak enjoys sex in
school. The Greaser would, too, if he were ever there.

The Jock is bisexual. There is, first of all, the
profound love he has for himself and his soggy blond
hair. And there is also his love for the prettiest girl
in school, head cheerleader Sally Ann Grand, whose
bouncing boobs made him throw eight interceptions
in one single game last year.

And speaking of boobs, the Nerd is interested in
them too. He just can't seem to find where they are.

Is It All Barnum and Bailey Now?

Because America has become one big drugstore, it is fitting to ask: in spite of the differences among these groups, is everyone now a Freak? The answer is yes and no, which is the kind of information you should be used to getting in this book.

The Freaks do the most drugs, of course—it is generally their major, along with organic farming and batik—but the three other Anti-Prep groups have been taking drugs as an elective. My investigation, conducted in depth during a lunch hour at a Fresno high school, has revealed:

The Jocks favor speed and painkillers before a game. After the game, they like to turn on with their own shaving lotion.

The Greasers, of course, prefer beer and selective sniffing of antifreeze.

And the Nerds turn on with Sinutabs.

Vacations

Anti-Preps often vacation close to Preps, but in dramatically different styles. For example, on the New Jersey shore, Preps go to big Victorian houses in Spring Lake, where they relax by sunbathing and excluding Jews. Anti-Preps, however, go to contemporary pizza stands in Asbury Park, where they have breakfast and then move on to a day of pinball and watching backsides go by.

The favorite Prep vacation spots, like Bar Harbor and Hilton Head, are well known. Anti-Prep spots are less publicized, primarily because Arnold Palmer never poses for pants in Jacob Riis Park.

Here, at last, is a semi-definitive list of the smartest Anti-Prep spas:

For the Greasers
The sections of Deal, New Jersey
marked for urban renewal

For the Freaks
The Kennedy Space Center

For the Jocks
Willis Reed's basketball clinic
at the Concord Hotel

For the Nerds
The computer room at Sesame Park

There's a small hotel
With a Lysol smell.

Pastimes

Just as a Prep is interested in learning how to tip and talk through his nose, an Anti-Prep has pastimes, too. You won't find them in *Town and Country,* but some of the following have gotten chic spreads in *Psychology Today.*

For the Greasers
Forging passes for skipping classes
Throwing beer cans in the school parking lot
Throwing up in the school parking lot

For the Jocks
Punching people on the arm
Squinting
Relaxing with a good book of Cliff notes

For the Freaks
Raising sesame seeds organically
Holding rallies for the Berrigans and Alger Hiss
Collecting early American coke spoons

For the Nerds
Memorizing famous chess moves
Celebrating National Library Week
Attending festivals of crop-dusting films

A Nerd relaxing with a good book.

Anti-Prep Music

It is common knowledge that a Prep's favorite song is either "Take Me Back to Nassau Hall" or "Doggie in the Window." Anti-Prep music, however, has an equally eloquent range.

The Freak Hit Parade
"Turning Japanese" by the Vapors
"Whip It" by the Moog Synthesizer
The Colombian National Anthem

The Greaser Hit Parade
"Ninety-Nine Bottles of Beer on the Wall"
by Joe Frazier
"Ave Maria" by Sha Na Na

The Nerd Hit Parade
The Theme from *Star Wars*
Stravinsky's *Rites of Spring*
"Where Is Thumbkin?"

The Jock Hit Parade
"The Star-Spangled Banner"

A budding Greaser at a chic resort.

Favorite Films

Greasers   *Rocky*
Freaks   *The Rocky Horror Show*
Jocks   *Knute Rockne—All American*
Nerds   *The Story of Rocks*

PHOTO QUIZ #4

Here is Photo Quiz #4. These are pictures of feet. All but one pair were photographed by Tom Dunham at a May Day parade in which he annually marches. See if you can identify the feet that are *not* Anti-Prep. If you happen to be a shoe salesman, a chiropodist, or a foot fetishist, please disqualify yourself.

101

LANGUAGE

Do Anti-Preps communicate as well as frogs?
Do they have as much to say?

Inspiration

Just as Preps are inspired by the words of Dina Merrill ("The Five and Ten? Is that a train?"), Anti-Preps also have words that stir them. Four of the most popular sayings follow. Note their wingéd brevity. It is hard for some of these people to remember more than six words.

For Jocks

Go for it!
　　Frank Gifford to his dog

For Nerds

I lost my lunch.
　　Galileo while searching for a brown bag

For Freaks

Into the toilet.
　　Jimmy the Greek on last week's game

For Greasers

So's your mother.
　　Cardinal Cooke to a Protestant friend

A jock likes to keep on top of things.

Diary of a Nerd

Last night I dreamed again about Nancy Reagan. I guess I'm in love with anything made by a computer.

Humor

Each of the Anti-Prep groups has its own unique sense of humor and can laugh heartily at things, just as a Prep likes to laugh at the latest knock-knock jokes.

(Knock-knock.

Who's there?

L. L. Bean.

L. L. Bean who?

L. L. Bean of Freeport, Maine.)

A Greaser's wit, for example, might take flight with his merrily saying to you, "Up yours with gauze," a bit of word play that he learned at his mother's knee.

A Freak, on the other hand, is not always quite as quick with a quip, perhaps because he swallowed his tongue a few minutes ago. But when they do manage to speak, Freaks like to spin humor with messages, jokes in which the punch line is nuclear contamination or red dye two.

(Can Communism protect its people from an outbreak of the plague?

No, during a plague the Red die too.)

For his humor, a Nerd sometimes likes to put his head inside a lampshade, which doesn't change his looks that much. A Jock, in contrast, has the subtlest sense of humor of all, so subtle that no one has ever been able to detect it with just the naked ear.

Alumni Newsletter

The Nerds of '59

Manny Creamer may or may not have been executed by Afghan tribesmen sometime after the Drexel game. Any 59ers with news of Manny—or anyone else shot by Moslems—drop us a line, okay?

Roger "Rog the Codg" Reeber writes, "Life in the First Methodist Church of Tyler, Texas, is pretty darn exciting these days. Along with all the christenings, burials, and pre-game prayers, I've also had some lively skirmishes with the Christian right, which I'd always thought was a slot formation at TCU. As for the gang at home, little Murray just started junior high and can't wait to be an orthodontist and Rhonda has started working at the blood bank. We were all pretty excited last week when she thought she'd found her first vein, but it turned out to be something else."

Arnie Snag reports, "Rhoda and I just bought a lovely condo in Managua, which we picked up for a song because we were lucky enough to follow both a revolution and an earthquake. No Dekes in Guatemala, even though everyone does get plenty of sack."

Cy "Sci Fi" Dopple offers this flash: "Life in the controller's office of the North Philadelphia branch of J. C. Penney can't compare to life at old RPI. In fact, nothing much has happened to Rona and me since the fall of '66, but we really can't complain because we do get out to the mall a lot. I don't see many of the guys from school, but I didn't see them at school either. One of our twins is getting her teeth straightened and the other her nose. We gave 'em their choice."

Lexicon

Part I: Traditional Speech

All four Anti-Prep groups have speech patterns that sometimes resemble English. Moreover, a word or phrase can have a certain meaning for one group and a different meaning for another, leading us to ask: who cares?

The answer is that from time to time, you may want to try communicating with a member of one of the groups. If so, then simply consult the following handy lexicon. I regret that there was no one at Wallaby who knew how to put this list in alphabetical order, but at least they did succeed in numbering the pages consecutively.

joint (n.) A marijuana cigarette; the place where two bones are attached; a sleazy club. Only the Jock has no meaning for this word. But when a Greaser, Freak, or Nerd says "You got a joint?" a fascinating ambiguity ensues, for he could mean "Have you got a marijuana cigarette?" or "Have you places where your bones are attached?" or "Have you a sleazy club?" Therefore, whenever the question is presented to you, be aware that you have a thirty-three percent chance of making sense—which may be your usual average anyway.

how they hanging? The meaning of this phrase
depends on the precise inflection with which it is
used. To a Greaser, "How they hanging?" usually
means, "Are they enjoying their comatose behavior
in the school parking lot?" The question, however,
could also show concern about the size of someone's
shorts.

the big O (n.) Once again, here is a phrase rich in
multi-directionality. To the Freak, *the big O* is an
orgasm; to the Jock, a shutout of his team; to the
Greaser, an oil change; and to the Nerd, an Oreo.

fuckin'-A (adj.) For all four groups (and Grace
Kelly, too), this phrase has nicely held a purity of
meaning: "I verify your data; consider yourself
resoundingly correct." *Fuckin'-A,* which received its
maximum usage in the Fort Dix motor pool in the
summer of 1958, is unfortunately starting to decline
and today is heard primarily in parochial schools
and state legislatures.

lube job (n? v?) To a Greaser, of course, this phrase
traditionally has meant to oil the parts of a car.
Lately, however, some Greasers also have been using
it to describe a woman in heat. ("Was it a lube job
for you, baby?") Therefore, lovers of both language
and lubrication now are worried that the new
meaning of the phrase could lead to confusion. For
example, "My mother had a lube job" could mean

either that she took the Toyota for servicing or that father serviced her.

bag it (v.) To a Greaser, Jock, or Freak, *bag it* means to stop an activity or cancel a plan. To a Nerd, it means to get dressed.

cheese out (v.) This phrase has fascinatingly antithetical meanings to all the groups, for it can refer to the passage of food in either direction. For example, "Did the queen cheese out?" can mean "Did the queen go out for pizza?" or "Did the pizza go out of the queen?"

Does a bear shit in the woods? A colorfully rhetorical question that to most Anti-Preps means "Can you have the slightest doubt that this is true?" At some urban schools, where students are unfamiliar with the habits of bears, the question becomes "Is the Pope a Catholic?" And at still other schools, an occasional Greaser is heard to say "Is a bear a Catholic?" or "Does the Pope shit in the woods?"

Lexicon

Part II: Modern Speech

The two most frequently used and fundamental thoughts—simultaneous on a bad night—of Anti-Preps are to have sex and to throw up. Anti-Preps are particularly creative in conceiving new language for these ancient rituals. In fact, all of the following phrases were coined the day before yesterday.

For Intercourse

Bring home the bacon
Bring home the bologna
Bury the bologna
Pass the pastrami
Go to Ontario
Go to Saskatchewan
Go to Detroit
Red light, green light, one-two-three
Step on your mother's back
Step on your mother's front

For Throwing Up

Bring home the bacon
Bring home the bacon, lettuce, and tomato
Go into reverse
Flunk emission control
Take another look at lunch

For Throwing Up During Intercourse
Dump on the hump

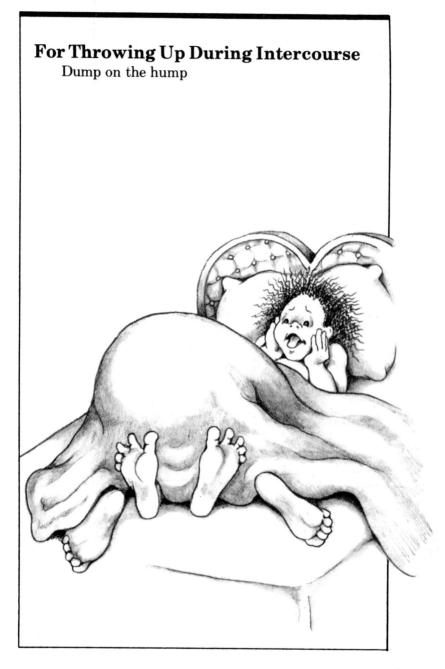

PHOTO QUIZ #5

All but one of these cars could be driven by Preps to Monhegan Island. That one is for Anti-Preps who vacation on Ellis Island. Which is it?

THE FUTURE

Is there a future to Anti-Prep?
Is there a past?
Is there a subjunctive?

Sic Semper Flatulentus

The Anti-Preps' equivalent of the Preps' Old Boy
Network is the Nerds' Young Weirdos Web. Since
Nerds have trouble talking to people, it was natural
for them to drift toward computers, where they are
slouched right now, playing games, popping pimples,
and planning nuclear strikes. World War III will not
match the American armed forces against the
Russian—it will match our Nerds against theirs. And
we can win if ours manage to remember which side
they are on.

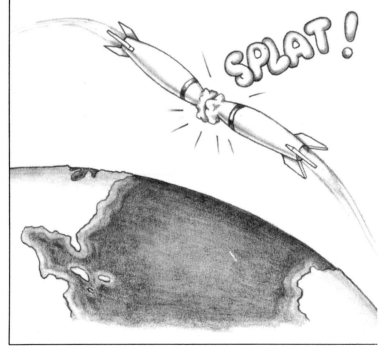

The Newest Nerds

The Japanese attack on American industry has been followed by their attack on the marking curves in American schools. The figures are dismaying and no protective tariff is in sight.

Sixty-eight percent of all high school valedictorians are now Japanese and the other thirty-two percent don't like the results of World War II.

"All Japanese are brilliant," American students keep telling me.

"Not *all*," I reply. "At Midway, Yamamoto was a schmuck."

It is now clear, however, that he was the *last* Japanese schmuck.